THE BEST
Paul Nicholls
BOOK IN THE WORLD...
EVER

Toby Reynolds

Paul Nicholls

First published in Great Britain in 1997 by Chameleon Books
an imprint of André Deutsch Ltd
106 Great Russell Street
London WC1B 3LJ
www.vci.co.uk

André Deutsch Ltd is a subsidiary of VCI plc.

The right of Toby Reynolds to be identified as the author of this
work has been asserted by him in accordance with the Copyright
Design and Patents Act, 1988.

ISBN 0 233 99285 5

Printed and bound in Great Britain by Butler and Tanner, Frome,
Somerset.

A catalogue record for this book is available from the British Library.

Contents

NAME: Paul Nich[...]
ORIGINAL NAME: [...]
Greenhaugh
DATE OF BIRTH: [...]
STAR SIGN: Arie[...]
[...]IGHT: [...]f[...]
[...]r: [...]
[...]UR: [...]
DI[...]INGUISHING [...]
Hairy chest, t[...]
bunny on right [...]
HOMETOWN: Bolt[...]
NOW LIVES: Buc[...]
FAVOURITE MUSI[...]

Paul N[...]

April 4, 1979

icholls

CHARAC CS:

ttoo boy

shoul

n, L e Ess

hurs reg—

: Hip-hop,

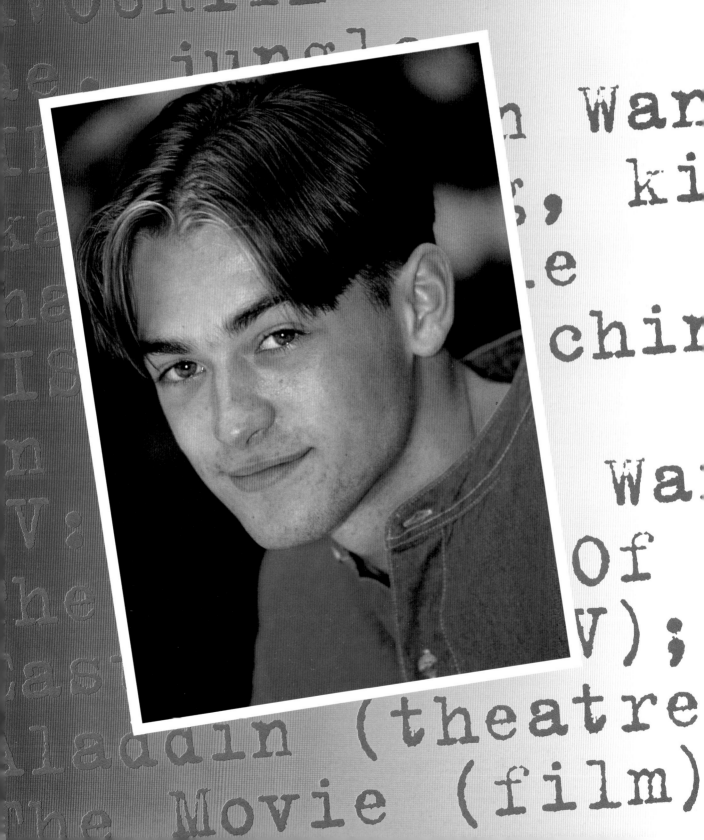

METOWN: Bolton,
LIVES: Buckhu
VOURITE MUSIC:
jungle
Wan
s, ki
le
chin

Wa
Of
V);
Aladdin (theatre
Movie (film)

fact file

NAME: Paul Nicholls
ORIGINAL NAME: Paul Gerald Greenhaugh
DATE OF BIRTH: April 4 1979
STAR SIGN: Aries
HEIGHT: 5 foot 10 inches
EYE COLOUR: Green
HAIR COLOUR: Light Brown
DISTINGUISHING CHARACTERISTICS:
Hairy chest, tattoo of Playboy bunny
on right shoulder
HOMETOWN: Bolton, Lancashire
NOW LIVES: Buckhurst Hill, Essex
FAVOURITE MUSIC: Hip-hop, reggae,
jungle
LIKES: Bolton Wanderers, acting,
skateboarding, kickboxing, Tupac
Shakur, Goldie
DISLIKES: Watching himself act on
TV, fame
CV: Children's Ward, Earthfast,
The Biz, Out Of The Blue, EastEnders
(TV); Blood Brothers, Aladdin
(theatre); Spice Girls: The Movie
(film)

Introduction

BE HONEST, would you have watched EastEnders as much in the past year or so if Paul Nicholls hadn't been in the cast? Nothing makes a soap worth watching like a fit man filling the screen. Who was fanciable before the arrival of Joe Wicks? Robbie Jackson has persistent spots. You wouldn't go out with Grant Mitchell unless you fancied your fat, balding uncle. And no-one is desperate enough to date Ian Beale.

When Joe Wicks turned up in Albert Square from his hometown of Bolton, the millions who had swooned over Paul in Children's BBC's The Biz knew that the soap's glumness rating was in for a swift downturn. Here was a rare babe living in a fictional area of London more used to the wrinkly faces of Dot and Ethel, the bad peroxides of Pauline Fowler and the terrible shirts of Nigel. There's just no contest in Walford to Joe's gorgeous eyes and floppy hair.

But Paul hasn't just made EastEnders 100% better looking. He has been involved in some tough, traumatic storylines, enough to tax the best acting skills of an established luvvie from the Royal Shakespeare Company, let alone a then 17-year-old making his first appearance on a primetime show. During his short time in the series, Joe has rediscovered his father, dodgy David Wicks, then lost him again. He has helped his best friend Sarah Hills out of a religious cult, then finally started going out with her after a year of wanting to be her boyfriend, coped with his loopy mother Lorraine's tumultuous love life, and all while suffering from severe mental illness.

The fact that he just happens to be drop dead as well is a major plus.

Joe Wicks makes the soap an absolute must-see. But Joe Wicks is only a convincing character because Paul Nicholls is such a brilliant actor. He manages to play Joe's condition with care, and doesn't just make us think he's slightly off his rocker. Paul's skill is in making Joe loveable, not just for his looks but for his funny and warm character as well. We would all be happy to do a better job than Lorraine in caring for someone like Joe.

Paul has the BBC at his feet. They know that we're watching the prog just to get a fix of Wicks. He could, if he wanted, sign up for a massive contract with the show, allowing him to stay in the soap forever and make pots of money. All very attractive, but Paul is much more sensible than that. He is taking care of

his career, because he has seen too many soap stars be massive one moment, then go down the dumper the next.

"I am in the top programme on TV right now," says Paul in his warm Northern accent that sounds so distinct in the cockney twang of Albert Square. "But you must never forget where you were before, and never be afraid to go back there."

But where was it that Paul Nicholls came from? What was he like as a kid, why did he become an actor, and why is he about to give it all up? The answers are here.

Welcome to the best Paul Nicholls book in the world ever....

Paul's family

Paul Nicholls was born **Paul Gerald Greenhaugh** in Bolton, on April 4 1979, to his mother, Julie, and his father, Paul Snr.

His sister Kelly had been born the year before. The family were to have no more children.

Paul had to get rid of the Greenhaugh (you say it Green-off, in case you were wondering) when he became an actor. **Not because he was embarrassed about the name,** but because of the strict laws that rule the theatrical profession. All actors have to join a union called Equity, but no two members of the union are allowed to have the same name. After all, there couldn't be two actors called Brad Pitt starring in the same film, could there? When Paul joined, there was already a Paul Greenhaugh on their books, so it was tough luck. Our lad had to change his name. He became Paul Nicholls.

He is proud of his family, and wouldn't have changed his name if it hadn't been for the necessities of work. He talks as much about going home to stay with his mum as he does about the celebrity life he leads in London.

Although he wouldn't miss the parties and the new friends he has made for the world, **his heart is still with his family** and old mates in Bolton. "I've not been brought up to be a star," he says. "It's flattering, but it's not what I'm about."

"I've not been brought up to be a star"

aaaah — isn't he luvverly? Paul and his mum on her birthday

His mum has meant more to him than just the usual support a son needs as he grows up. She was the inspiration for him becoming an actor rather than a footballer for his beloved Bolton Wanderers. When Julie was Paul's age, she won a place to study at the Royal Academy of Dramatic Arts, or RADA, in London, the prestigious college which lists great actors among its former pupils. But just before she was due to leave for the college, tragedy struck. "Mum won a place at RADA but just before she was due to go my Grandad had an accident and they couldn't afford to send her," says Paul.

"My mum never regretted it but what happened to her has given me a real drive to get on. I learned that you only have one chance at these things and you have to grab them as they come along."

It was not the end of Julie's acting, and she has appeared in TV shows and on adverts, but she never made enough to

earn a living, and found work as a psychiatric nurse. This job, put together with her acting experience, has been helpful to Paul as he prepared for the role of the mentally disturbed Joe. His mum gave him insights into how a person with such a problem would be handled in the real world. "Mum's been brilliant," Paul says. "She didn't push me to get into this business. It was my decision and she supported me."

Paul keeps his feet on the ground by going back to Bolton, where he tries to forget about the pressures of fame. "When I visit my family," he says, "I don't talk about work, they'd get bored listening."

Sadly, his parents have recently separated, the story making lurid head-lines in the tabloid newspapers in March, 1997. It is this sort of intrusion into his life that makes Paul hate his new position. "I love acting, but I hate being famous," he admits. Unfortunately, when you are in a soap, it is hard to have one without the other. No wonder Paul decided to quit the Square.

"When I visit my family, I don't talk about work – they'd get bored listening."

PAUL WAS A PUPIL at the Church Road Primary School in Bolton, then at Smithhills Dean High School. He was a bit of a swot, leaving school with seven GCSEs, including an "A" in drama, but `there were two extra-curricular activities that interested him much more than the classroom. There was the football pitch, and there was the stage.`

When he was nine, he started out on the first of his two career options, by joining a local kids' team called the Grasshoppers. He was good on the pitch, and has always enjoyed the game. But there was something else tugging him away from football.

Paul first appeared on stage at the age of nine, in his primary school production of Aladdin. It may not sound much of a start. We're all made to appear in school plays at Christmas and we don't become actors. But it was here that Paul first got his taste for the profession. "Acting is all I've ever dreamed of since I appeared in a play at primary school," he remembers. Less than ten years later, he was to star in Aladdin again. But this time it was to rave reviews, in a big budget version in Chatham, Kent, at Christmas 1996.

School productions were soon not enough to satisfy Paul. He managed to get a small part on the Children's ITV drama, Children's Ward, it was only three lines, but it was enough to spur on his ambitions. After he left primary school, he joined the Oldham Theatre Workshop so that he could learn the tricks of the trade amongst other budding actors. "When I started at the Oldham Theatre Workshop, I was eleven and quite ambitious. I always believed in myself," says Paul. But acting, and the increased attention Paul received, had its downside. He was bullied.

"My first year at Secondary school was really tough. Other pupils expected me to be really arrogant and egotistical and they took the mickey out of me. They used to tell me I was a rubbish actor. I got into a few fights because of it."

a kid

Anyone who's been bullied knows how awful it is. Paul could have bowed to their pressure, and stopped acting just to stop the taunts. But the abuse only proved to himself how much he wanted to stick to his dreams. Even with the taunts, he entered, and won, a national award for public speaking at the age of 12. "At the time it was awful, but now I think it made me a stronger person," he recalls. "I learned how to handle myself and it made me realise just how much I wanted to act. It was only when I was acting that I was really happy."

The Oldham Theatre Workshop doesn't sound like the ideal launchpad for a massive career, but it was from here that Paul was thrown into the spotlight, when, at the age of thirteen, he was spotted by a talent scout.

"They used to tell me I was a rubbish actor. I got into a few fights because of it."

Guess who?

At the age of nine, Paul wanted to be a footballer, so he joined a local kids' team, the Grasshoppers. Luckily for us, he is a better actor than a footballer.

Paul's

girls

But don't worry. It wasn't all hard work and trouble for Paul. He'd got his m_tes who stuck by him before he became famous – the sign of really good friends. When he wasn't on stage or playing football, he was out having a laugh, looking for a girl. "When I w_s young," Paul says, "I was like all t_ _ other lads, trying to get off with different girls every night. But then I fell in love and everything changed."

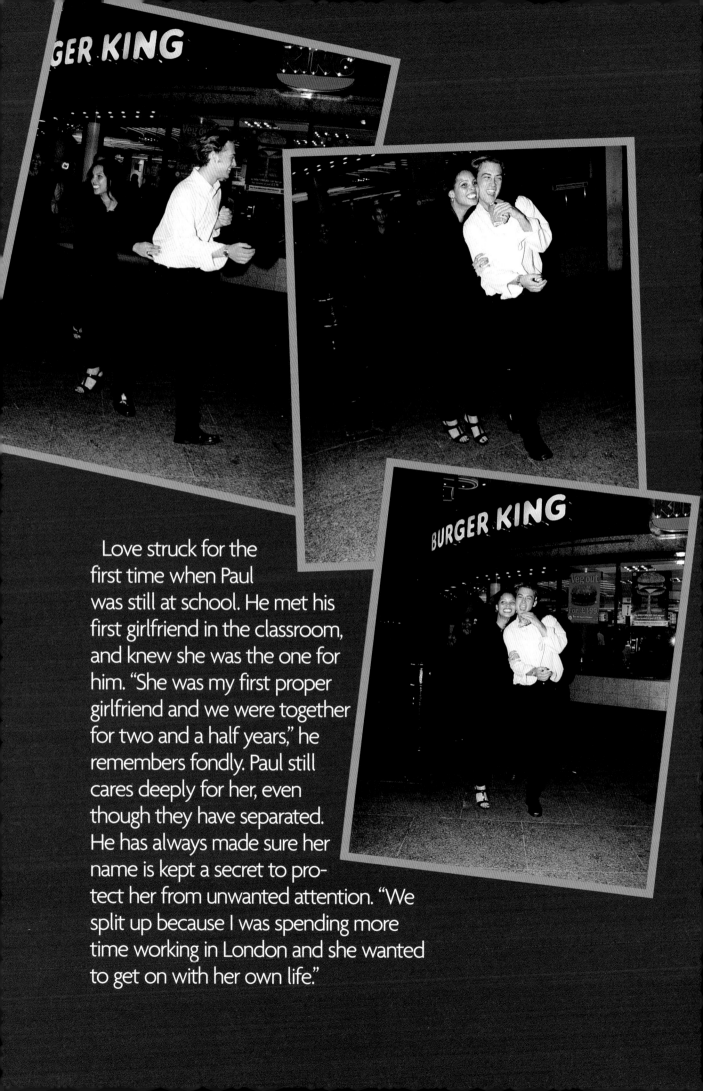

Love struck for the first time when Paul was still at school. He met his first girlfriend in the classroom, and knew she was the one for him. "She was my first proper girlfriend and we were together for two and a half years," he remembers fondly. Paul still cares deeply for her, even though they have separated. He has always made sure her name is kept a secret to protect her from unwanted attention. "We split up because I was spending more time working in London and she wanted to get on with her own life."

But what does Paul like in a girl? Of course, he likes it if they are a babe. You only have to see his current girlf, model Joanna Clark, to realise that. But more importantly, he wants someone who is caring and understanding. Even though he's got a cocky way with words and likes to party, Paul is really very quiet and sensitive. "I really don't understand girls," he admits.

"In fact, I'm a shy person. All I really want is a hug."

He had his fair share of running around when he was a kid, but now yearns for the sort of commitment he found first time round. "I really did love her and I've been looking for those kind of feelings ever since we split," he says. "Until I do I just couldn't enjoy being with another girl and I'm not interested in one-night stands because I know how much better it feels when you're in love."

He'd make a perfect boyfriend, waiting for the right girl before rushing in head first. "My house-mates are always taking the mickey out of me for not making the most of all the offers I get from fans. They even asked me if I was gay because I've never brought a girl home. Of course I'm not. I just don't want to leap into bed with someone I don't care about."

His love life has been much like Joe Wicks', waiting for the right girl to come along. Of course, Joe ended up with Sarah Hills, and now Paul has struck gold, head over heels with Joanna Clark. Sorry, girls, but that's the way things are. He's taken.

"They even asked me if I was gay because I've never brought a girl home. Of course I'm not. I just don't want to leap into bed with someone I don't care about."

Paul's 1st

WHEN PAUL STARTED at the Oldham Theatre Workshop, he did not expect it to lead to the first of many major roles on TV. He knew he wanted to act as a career, but he had no idea his dreams would come true so soon, and with such an incredible reaction.

But the talent scout who dropped in on the workshop one weekend knew Paul had the looks and talent to make him a star. He was quickly snapped up by the BBC to take the lead role in Earthfast, a spooky drama which saw Paul performing yet another role that made him appear slightly mad.

Paul starred as David who, with his friend Keith (played by Chris Downs), go and investigate weird noises they hear coming from inside a hill. The hill opens, and out of it comes a drummer boy who believes he is in the eighteenth century (kinda like Joe Wicks thinking Grant Mitchell was going to come out of Peggy's TV set). It turns out the drummer is searching for King Arthur, and soon returns to his own time, but leaves behind a candle. David (that's Paul) becomes obsessed with this candle, as you would if it was given to you by a 200-year-old boy who's just walked out of a hill. He starts to act a bit strangely, then suddenly disappears in a flash of lightening. Everyone thinks he's dead, but he has only been transported back to another time, and eventually solves a mystery involving King Arthur, even getting to meet the monarch himself.

It's not quite on a par with the drama of Joe and his alien-conquering Bacofoil, but then it was for kids' TV. And although the series didn't turn him into a celebrity straight away, Paul caught the imagination of thousands of female viewers. After he started on Earthfast, he received 3,000 fan letters. 'Mostly they were from girls asking for advice about boyfriends and stuff, but I'm not in a position to give advice, am I?'

TV jobs

"I was only young and not very experienced with girls and stuff."

This was sadly the case. Paul was having to spend long periods away from Bolton to film Earthfast. He was forced to decide between his work and his love life. However, the opportunities that he knew were just around the corner made him commit himself to his career and leave behind his girlf.

Of course, the show that really catapulted Paul into mass babe-dom was The Biz, the smash hit series from Children's BBC. On the screens in Spring 1995, it was about young hopefuls who were desperate to make it big. Paul played Tim, one of these wannabes who had just returned to the Markov Academy of Dance and Drama after appearing in a big budget Hollywood film that was about to be released in the UK.

In the series, his character had to cope with massive attention from the newspapers, which turned out to be incredibly prophetic of Paul's real future. At the time, however, he didn't have to put up with those pressures. 'I'm not what you'd call famous yet, am I?' he said at the time. 'And I can't imagine being in a position where acting is a strain. It's all I've wanted to do since I appeared in that school play at primary school - it's a bit of a buzz. I don't mind being recognised in the street although it hasn't reached Sean Maguire proportions yet!

How times have changed. Sean Maguire is down the dumper, and now Paul is the one with all the attention. The Biz caught on because it was so realistic. 'Of course, I never went to a stage school like this one,' Paul explains, 'but other people who've been to stage schools have told me that the series is very true to life. I watched some episodes of Fame [dodgy US drama about a stage school] and I just couldn't believe it. I mean, everything was going on there and I don't think that happens in real life. This show dealt much more with what's involved in the professional side of becoming an actor.'

The job was made even better because he had to get down and dirty in love scenes with co-star Stephanie Bagshaw, who played Sasha, the one in the show who didn't want to become an actress, but was being forced into it by her pushy mother who worked at the school and was always arranging unwarranted interviews for her. 'I've, erm, never done a love scene before,' he said at the time, just before the scenes were due to be shot. 'I hope it goes alright. Still, snogging is a nice way to earn money, isn't it?'

Paul loved the experience of The Biz. He was now certain that acting was the career for him. As well as The Biz, there were other jobs which confirmed his skills. He appeared on stage in the musical Blood Brothers, and played the part of a young father accused of murdering his baby in the harrowing BBC drama series Out Of The Blue. All this while he was still committed to seeing through his GCSE exams back home in Bolton.

I've, erm, never done a love scene before,

he said at the time, just before the scenes were due to be shot.

I hope it goes alright. Still, snogging is a nice way to earn money, isn't it?

Joe

fact file

NAME: Joe Wicks
AGE: 15 in 1996
BIRTHPLACE: Bolton,
Lancashire
NOW LIVES: 47 Albert Square,
Walford, London E20
PARENTS: David and Lorraine
Wicks
BROTHERS AND SISTERS: One
sister, Karen, killed in a
car crash
GIRLFRIEND: Sarah Hills
LIKES: Grant Mitchell,
Manchester United, Bacofoil,
sticky tape, Sarah Hills
DISLIKES: Grant Mitchell,
aliens, his tablets, school
CV: working in the cellar of
the Queen Vic, polishing cars
at Deals On Wheels, helping
Nigel in his video store

WICKS

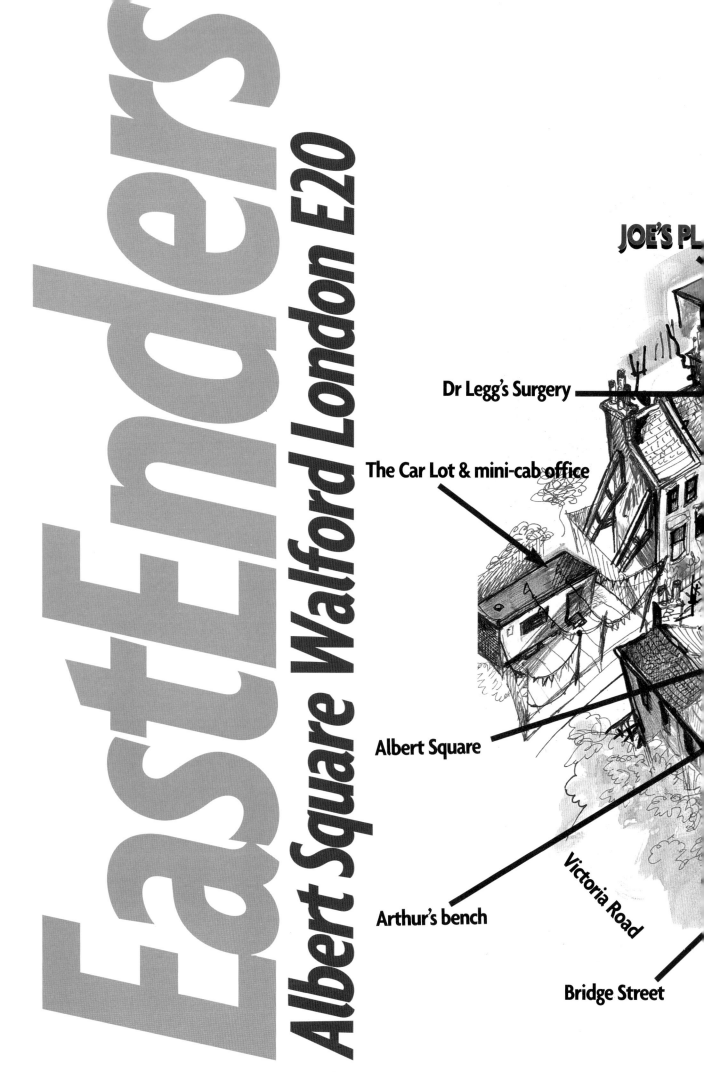

EastEnders

Albert Square Walford London E20

JOE'S PL

Dr Legg's Surgery

The Car Lot & mini-cab office

Albert Square

Victoria Road

Arthur's bench

Bridge Street

Joe Wicks
— a short

EVEN THOUGH he was about to start work on the hottest programme on British TV, Paul was more cocky than scared. 'When I started,' he says, 'I didn't have time to be nervous, because I was on the set the day after being told I'd got the part of Joe. The thing is, I didn't follow EastEnders avidly. I just treated it like any other job.'

And so 17-year-old Paul swanned into Albert Square, as if he were unaware that the role he was taking would put his face in 20 million front rooms three times a week. He treated the work with ease, as if he were just helping his dad out with a roofing job, as he has done in his breaks from acting.

But it was inevitable that he would be so unfazed. He had won the part so quickly, there wasn't time for the reality of the situation to sink in. He had auditioned on Monday, heard he'd clinched the part on Tuesday, and was on the set of the Square the very next day, plunged straight into the traumatic role of Joe Wicks.

In his debut episode, broadcast on Monday March 25, 1996, no-one in the Square knew the identity of the mysterious teenager seen lurking around Walford. Whilst the rest of the residents are cooing over Kathy and Phil's new baby, and Mark is still trying to free Arthur Fowler from prison, the stranger seems to be looking for David Wicks, but doesn't appear to be having much success since Dirty David is more interested in shacking up with Cindy Beale. In the next episode, Cindy and David are having a sordid quickie in the Deals On

Joe Wicks
history

Wheels portakabin when they hear a noise outside. They rush out, and see the back of the stranger running off. Dopey Nigel gets a better view, and says he'd be able to recognise him again.

The stranger is back on the car lot that night, breaking into one of the vehicles and getting some sleep on the back seat. The next day, and also the following episode, the unknown character goes to the Cafe to try and get some food, but he only has 20p left. Kind-hearted Blossom gives him a burger and some tea anyhow, and starts to ask the teenager some questions – whether he has any family, won't they be worried about him, that sort of thing. All the kid reveals is that this is his first time in London.

that boy?

Naughty
David

While they are talking, Nigel comes into the cafe, sees the boy and runs to get David. David comes over, Nigel grabs the kid who is trying to run away. But David recognises the face straight away, tells Nigel to let the boy go, then walks away. But the boy comes after him and calls David 'Dad'. The secret is revealed, we discover the boy's name is Joe, and the tense and troubled relationship between father and son is started as it means to go on. It turns out that David had married Lorraine Wicks when he was still a teenager. They had two children together, Joe and Karen. But while Lorraine had wanted a family, David wanted to play the field and go out every night. When Joe was 8 and Karen was 6, David had got bored and left the family. He hadn't spoken to Lorraine since, not having any contact with them for eight years.

He didn't even know that his daughter Karen had been killed in a car crash nine months before.

David didn't want them plaguing his life now he was successful both in work and love – after a shaky start on the Square trying to take over his late father Pete Beale's vegetable stall, he had got Cindy Beale under his thumb, and was now making a mint at Deals On Wheels with his mother Pat Butcher and his step-brother Ricky.

But it wasn't to go how David wanted. Joe had run away to London to try and find his father, traumatised by the loss of his sister and the lack of attention from his mum. He seemed to be coping well with the situation when he first hit Walford, but little did we know these events, and the cold reaction of David to his long-lost son, would be the trigger for Joe's disturbing mental illness, schizophrenia.

Wicks' son

how paul felt about eastenders

OFF-SCREEN, the relationship between Paul and his colleagues started on much firmer ground. 'Michael French, who played my Dad, and Pam St Clements, who plays Pat, soon put me at ease,' remembers Paul, 'I've learned a lot about acting since I started on the show. But Joe's character was pretty easy to fall into because we're both very similar. We're both insecure, so people get to us, and we care what friends think.'

It was obvious the programme needed a babe to draw in a new audience. The main plot of the time, David and Cindy, was certainly juicy, what with Cindy's plans to leave the Square with David and her three children, but the soap lacked a vital spark. With Arthur Fowler's arrest over the missing 'Flowering Wilderness' money dragging on forever, EastEnders needed some oomph to get it going again – it needed a total pin-up.

Paul proved to be what the programme lacked. He is now the only member of the cast ever to have had their own personal fan club. He gets 500 letters every week. But Paul has had to do more than just turn up and look pretty. The role of Joe Wicks was more than just that of an awkward adolescent. From the start, Joe has been isolated from most of the other characters in the Square, always involved in intense storylines, rarely getting any light relief, or a girlfriend. Sorry Paul, but there's been little snogging in Albert Square. He has had to do some serious preparation for the role.

'People say it must, be hard playing Joe,' he says, but it was worse at the beginning. It was easier when the scripts showed how far gone he is.

'I wondered whether I should play him normal, with his illness coming on suddenly. In the end, I worked in a few little things which gradually showed his vulnerability and trauma.

'Because Joe is so intense I thought having physical characteristics would help me get into the role,' Paul continues. 'As he is so confused a slight facial twitch seemed a good idea and I also wring my hands to make him look disturbed. As the role became heavier I decided to carry on with Joe's characteristics even when I wasn't filming, so that when I did have to switch back into character it wouldn't be so difficult.'

But this commitment has proved troublesome. Paul seemed to become so wrapped up in the part that he was accused of suffering from mental problems himself, something he strongly denies. 'The truth is that the part hasn't got to me. It's just that when I was playing Joe I found it easier to stay in character all day until I left the studio. All that other stuff is a load of rubbish. Anyway, I hope my character doesn't take me over!

Paul's brilliant performance didn't just gain praise from critics and fans. He was praised by experts in the mental health profession, too. 'There are thousands of people watching EastEnders who know somebody like Joe,' says Gary Hogman of the National Schizophrenia Fellowship. 'For the character with the most fan mail to develop schizophrenia is a fantastic opportunity for people to see what the illness is really about.'

However proud he was of his performance in the show, Paul was afraid of EastEnders overshadowing him as an actor. There is nothing worse than to be typecast, especially when you are not yet even 20. Paul has realised he needs to break away from the series now. He wants people to recognise his talent in making Joe Wicks come to life, but he never wants people to forget that he, Paul Nicholls, is a totally separate person.

THE BEST
Paul Nicholls
BOOK IN THE WORLD...
EVER

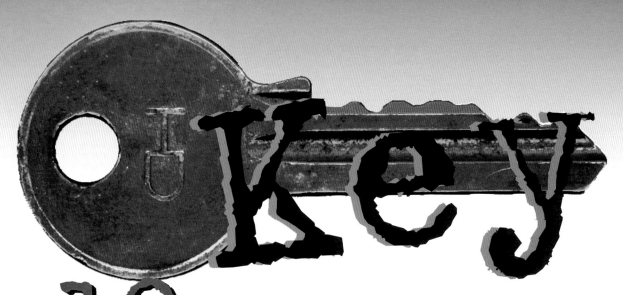

Key

The 10 episodes of EastEnders every **true Paul Nicholls fan** will never forget.

KISSIN' IN THE BACK ROW

Episode 341: Broadcast Tuesday June 11, 1996

Joe, who has just discovered that Bianca Jackson is his half-sister, takes Sarah Hills on their first date. They go to the cinema, but when Joe tries to kiss her, she stops him and runs inside. Joe thinks she doesn't like him, but the truth is Sarah is so confused by her strict religious cult she only knows she needs Joe as her one reliable friend. It is not until over a year later that the two finally get together.

EVERYBODY HATES ME

Episode 378: Broadcast Monday September 2, 1996

Joe is heading for the deep end. He has just got back from Blackpool, where he spent the time freaking out in an arcade at the mechanical laughing clowns while Tony was getting off with Simon for the first time on the pier. Now he is acting stranger than ever, freaking out when he goes for lunch at his gran Pat Butcher's house, telling Pat to mind her own business when she tries to talk to him. His half-uncle Ian Beale tells David that he should sack Joe from Deals On Wheels because of his bad behaviour, but when David has a word with his son Joe goes off on one, saying David hates him, that everyone hates him, and that they are all against him. David tries to comfort him, but it is too little, too late. David is doing a fine job of becoming the worst father EVER to appear in a soap.

EastEnders Episodes

EVIL

Episode 401: Broadcast Thursday October 24, 1996

The infamous EVIL episode. David tries to make Joe have a bath and go to school, but Joe, who hasn't washed for days, says no, because he claims he has to stay at home and "collect information". He stares at the blank TV screen, but, David being David, is too wrapped up in his own affairs to be bothered to stay and look after him. Throughout the day on his own, Joe is too scared to pick up the phone. Sarah eventually persuades him to come to the cafe, but he refuses to sit with his back to the door, and doesn't take his eye off it as he rocks back and forwards. He then asks Sarah if she fancies him, she says not like that, but he forces himself on her and snogs her roughly. She runs out, and Alistair, Sarah's creepy cult leader who has seen the whole affair taking place, says what Joe did was evil. Big mistake, as Joe totally wigs out, runs home, grabs a marker pen then writes E-V-I-L in big letters across his bare chest. Uh-oh.

PLAYING WITH FIRE

Episode 404: Broadcast Thursday October 31, 1996

Things go from worse to terrible. Joe thinks that Grant is Satan, ever since he saw Grant trash David's flat in an attempt to teach David a lesson. But Lorraine persuades Grant and Peggy, Grant's mother, to let Joe stay at the Queen Vic with them. They agree, even though Grant says that Joe is 'one sandwich short of a picnic.' Everyone goes to a fireworks display, but Joe sneaks away early. When his mum goes to find him, she sees Joe in the sitting room at the Vic, covered in lighter fuel and playing with matches. Grant tries to reason with him, but David, who has been off secretly shagging Carol, arrives and Joe tells his father that Satan is in the room. Joe asks David if he will protect him from all evil, and David says yes, a bad move as it locks him into Joe's mind games. Joe hands him back the matches, and Dr Legg arrives, telling them Joe needs to see a psychiatrist. It is the first time the parents are told to seek medical help.

ACE OF SPADES

Episode 408: Broadcast Monday November 11, 1996

The one with the TV and the window ledge. Peggy goes into her sitting room, to find the TV completely wrapped up in brown sticky tape. Turns out Joe did it because he thinks Grant is telling him to do bad things, talking to him through the TV, and that soon 'they' are going to come and get him, drag him away and torture him. Lorraine is terrified by this and locks Joe in the kitchen. David comes and lets him out, but now Joe thinks Lorraine is evil too. David takes him back to the flat, where Joe goes to sleep. David thinks it is safe to pop out for a quicky with Carol, but Joe wakes up alone and loses it. The phone rings, so Joe cuts the wire. The mobile rings, so he smashes it, then puts Motorhead's The Ace Of Spades on at top volume while he curls up into a ball. Next-door neighbour Kathy Mitchell bangs on the wall, but this only frightens Joe more. He opens the window and climbs out, desperate to escape. Der-der-der-der-der-der-der goes the theme music. Doh!

IN MY ROOM

Episode 410: Broadcast Thursday November 14, 1996

David is looking for a pair of scissors that should be in the kitchen drawer. He thinks they must be in Joe's room, which Joe has banned him from entering, always keeping the door firmly locked. But Joe is asleep on the sofa, so David slips the key from his pocket and opens the door. The room is plastered wall to

wall with graffiti, newspaper cuttings and photos. The words say evil, fear, Satan and devil, the stories are from the paper, all about crashes and disasters. David finally sees the reality of Joe's mental problems that have been staring him in the face.

FOILED AGAIN

Episode 414: Broadcast Monday November 25, 1996

At the end of the episode before this one, David fled the Square forever, terrified of being linked to the shooting of Ian Beale, arranged by partner in passion Cindy Beale. Joe has now locked himself up in the flat, and eventually the landlord calls the police to break the lock after Lorraine can't persuade Joe to open the door. They find the rooms in a complete state, entirely covered in tin foil to stop 'them'. When Joe doesn't recognise his own mother and starts talking about going to get chips for his dead sister Karen, the police decide to call a psychiatrist. Finally Joe is about to get some treatment, even though Lorraine is reluctant, stupidly thinking he is just upset about David. He agrees to go to outpatients the next day only after Nigel lends him one of his gross Hawaiian shirts, the patterns of which apparently jam alien frequencies.

THE DEVIL COMES FOR XMAS

Episode 427a: Broadcast Wednesday
December 25, 1996

At the end of the previous night's episode Joe, who is out of hospital but not taking his pills, found Lorraine snogging Grant in the Vic, even though Grant is now married to Tiffany. At Christmas lunch the next day, Grant is about to carve the turkey. But as he picks up the knife, Joe grabs Lorraine and shouts, 'Watch out, get away from there. He's the devil!' Everyone looks embarrased, but Joe carries on. He says if Grant isn't the devil, then why was he kissing Lorraine last night? Tiffany, who is pregnant with a baby that could turn out to be Grant's, looks at him furiously, then storms out. Joe goes upstairs and pours all his pills out of the window.

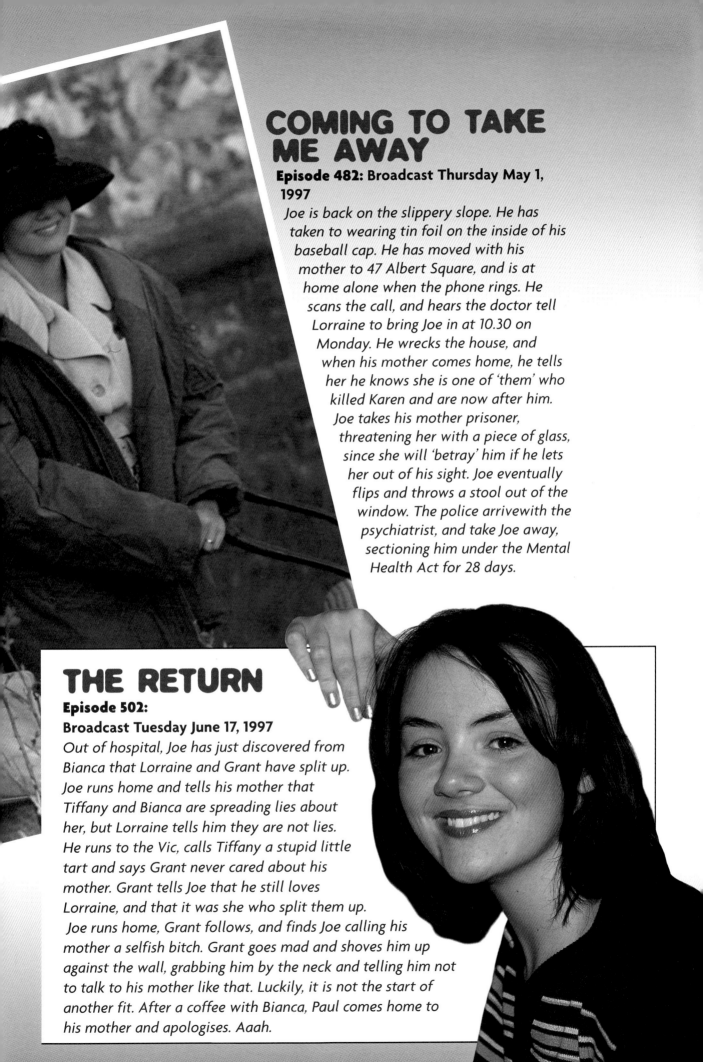

COMING TO TAKE ME AWAY

Episode 482: Broadcast Thursday May 1, 1997

Joe is back on the slippery slope. He has taken to wearing tin foil on the inside of his baseball cap. He has moved with his mother to 47 Albert Square, and is at home alone when the phone rings. He scans the call, and hears the doctor tell Lorraine to bring Joe in at 10.30 on Monday. He wrecks the house, and when his mother comes home, he tells her he knows she is one of 'them' who killed Karen and are now after him. Joe takes his mother prisoner, threatening her with a piece of glass, since she will 'betray' him if he lets her out of his sight. Joe eventually flips and throws a stool out of the window. The police arrivewith the psychiatrist, and take Joe away, sectioning him under the Mental Health Act for 28 days.

THE RETURN

Episode 502:

Broadcast Tuesday June 17, 1997

Out of hospital, Joe has just discovered from Bianca that Lorraine and Grant have split up. Joe runs home and tells his mother that Tiffany and Bianca are spreading lies about her, but Lorraine tells him they are not lies. He runs to the Vic, calls Tiffany a stupid little tart and says Grant never cared about his mother. Grant tells Joe that he still loves Lorraine, and that it was she who split them up. Joe runs home, Grant follows, and finds Joe calling his mother a selfish bitch. Grant goes mad and shoves him up against the wall, grabbing him by the neck and telling him not to talk to his mother like that. Luckily, it is not the start of another fit. After a coffee with Bianca, Paul comes home to his mother and apologises. Aaah.

THERE SEEM TO BE two views of Paul and how he spends his time away from the Square. On one side, some people have accused him of underage drinking when he was still 17, and linked him to a string of girls and wild parties. But then there is the other side, the shy and insecure Paul, who's like his character on the soap, commited to his girlfriend, likes a drink but doesn't have too much. Obviously, the real picture is to be found somewhere in the middle.

The best example of this was when Paul did Christmas panto in 1996, starring as the Genie Of The Ring (wearing the skimpiest costume you have ever seen) in Aladdin. The show was a massive hit, with other local pantos closing down because his show was so popular. But after the curtain had fallen for the night, there were tales of Paul drinking bars dry around the town. 'He always has a full pint of Fosters in his hand. He never danced, in fact he never left the bar,'

said Mark Hegarty, the DJ in one of the clubs called Excaliburs. The crowds of girls that followed him around were so determined that he even had to hire his own bodyguard, Paula Hanson. Sounds like Paul is a total party animal.

But this isn't the whole picture. He did have the odd drink at Christmas, but it was hardly the 'three week bender' as it was described by some papers. 'The reports of illegal drinking sessions are absolute rubbish,' he says. 'I only went out twice during the whole pantomime run and didn't get drunk once.' This sounds closer to the truth than the tabloids would like to think. Recently, Paul had lunch with colleagues at the BBC. Apparently, they were all drinking alcohol, but Paul had nothing stronger than a Coke.

That doesn't mean he doesn't know how to enjoy himself. 'We're always talking about career moves,' he says, 'But all I've been doing is going out and getting drunk.' He bears the mark – literally – of a night when he was apparently slightly tipsy – there is a tattoo on his right shoulder of the Playboy bunny, in honour of the late rapper Tupac Shakur, a man who was covered in similar tats.

Since Paul started on EastEnders, he has gained freedom in the capital that he had never known before.

Out of school, and with a starting salary of £65,000 which soon rose to £80,000, he could easily afford to have a good time. He's often out largin' it, especially at clubs like the Hanover Grand, partying with Sid Owen or Martine McCutcheon.

He's also tried to dump a load of his old jeans and sweaters for some designer gear. 'When I first came to London, I was invited to loads of parties and premieres. I thought I could just turn up in jeans and trainers. Fortunately my flatmates took me in hand. They ordered me to wear a suit and leave my trainers at home.'

He hasn't totally changed his look, though – he still likes sports stuff, it's just that he's just upgraded the labels. 'I like casual styles and tend to pick up trainers and stuff at shops like JD Sports. I've also bought a few designer things such as Armani jeans and a Polo Ralph Lauren jumper. My biggest buy was a new Moschino suit. It's black, cost £250, and it's the most I've ever spent on clothes.'

But he's still sentimental about his old stuff. It means too much to him to throw it all away. 'I'm still just a Bolton lad at heart. While it's nice to look good, I'm just as comfy in my old jeans and a T-shirt.'

He lives in Essex, in easy reach of the West End, sharing a house with Martine and another friend. But even though he has traded his hometown for London, he still hasn't lost his roots - Bolton Wanderers. He hasn't changed allegiance to Arsenal or any other London team, and he hasn't started to support Joe Wicks' team of choice. 'I hate having to wear a Manchester United shirt on EastEnders,' he says. 'My mates back home give me such flak about it.'

But there is one thing over which his

Paul's fave rave
Tupac Shakur factFILE

Name? Tupac Shakur (also spelt 2Pac)

Real Name? Errrm, really, it s Tupac Shakur

So what does Tupac mean? HIs mother was a member of the Black Panthers, a hard-line, black militant group that fought against racism in America in the Sixties and Seventies. Tupac was named after a warrior, the last Inca chief to be tortured and murdered by Spanish conquistadors. Shakur was like a clan name for the black nationalists in New York

Occupation? Superstar rapper, his biggest hit was California Love. He was also a brilliant actor, his best film being Gridlock d

Age? 25, and forever 25. He was sadly shot dead on September 7 1996 in Las Vegas, USA, after watching a title fight by Mike bite Tyson. He died in hospital on September 13, 1996

Who by? No-one knows for sure who was behind the drive-by shooting, but Tupac was involved in a bitter war between the rap communities of America s East and West coasts. Tupac s Los Angeles based label, Death Row, had become the bitter enemy of Sean Puffy Combes New York based label, Bad Boy Entertainment. The heated verbal exchanges had turned to violence. Tupac s camp believes their New York rivals were behind Tupac s death

Can this really be true? Tupac s main enemy was rapper the Notorious B.I.G.. Tellingly, six months after Shakur s death, Notorious was also murdered. It is hard not to see Notorious s death as some sort of retribu-tion

So what about these tattoos? Mr Shakur enjoyed painting his skin. As he became more obsessed with gang life, his torso become covered with tattoos. He had one saying, 50 NIGGAZ, which stood for Never Ignorant Getting Goals Accomplished. There was a gun in the centre of his chest, and the words THUG LIFE in big letters stretching over his belly. The I in LIFE was in the shape of a bullet

If he was so obsessed with gangs, doesn't that make him a bit dodgy? Not necessarily. It is hard for us in the UK to understand how hard life is in America s poor black communities. Although Tupac had been involved in gang violence, at the time of his assassination, he was trying to escape the lifestyle. His bravest step was his attempt to leave Death Row records, a company with strong links to the brutal gang lifestyle. Some have gone as far as to suggest that Suge Knight, Death Row s boss, was behind Tupac s death, punishing him for wanting to leave the label. However, since Tupac was sitting beside Knight, in his boss s BMW when the shooting occurred (Knight was slightly wounded), it seems unlikely

So what's the big deal? Imagine if Liam and Noel Gallagher were both murdered — that is the severity of the situation in rap music now. Many hope the deaths will lead to peace between the gangsta rappers of New York and Los Angeles. But the depth of feeling in both camps means this longed for compromise will proba-bly never happen

2PAC

california love

featuring dr dre

joanna clark

In February 1997, Paul was photographed sitting on a park bench, not snogging with a young blonde woman, but getting fresh all the same. They laughed and joked, then cuddled as they stood up. The woman he was with was Daniela Denby-Ashe, the actress who plays Sarah Hills in EastEnders.

But the Sunday Mirror, which reported this story, had got the wrong end of the stick. The pair had actually been photographed in character, preparing to film the scenes in EastEnders when Sarah has run away after she discovers the truth about creepy Alistair and his religious cult. In real life, Paul wasn't seeing Daniela. 'Romance, you must be joking!' Daniela says. 'I thought I looked horrendous in that photo because of my dirty, greasy hair! Paul and I had a really great laugh about it because it wasn't true anyway, and I looked terrible in the pictures. It was just part of the storyline that was mistaken for real life romance.' Anyway, another blonde had just entered his life, and it was clear that she was much more romantically interesting to Paul.

Joanna Clark, a model his age, has turned out to be just the love that Paul has been searching for all these years. They have been dating since the start of 1997, and often take intimate breaks away together. The couple spent Valentine's Day at the luxury health farm Henlow Grange, with Sid Owen and his girlfriend Lucy Slater. He celebrated his 18th birthday by whisking Joanna off to Paris, the most romantic city in the world. Do you know a better boyfriend?

Makes you sick.

After they returned to the country, Paul threw a party at the cool Hacienda club in Manchester, taking over the Freak bar to celebrate his 18th with 200 of his friends. Until then, Paul had tried to keep Joanna a secret, but now he was happy to show off his new love, smooching in the corner without a care in the world.

aaaaaaaaaa

aaahhh!!!

Asked to make a speech, he stood up and proclaimed, 'All I want to say is Bollocks.' Fair enough. As he left the club, supported by Joanna, he was heard to say, 'I feel sick. I'm going home.' And who doesn't on their 18th birthday?

help me

eeee!!!!!

As well as caring for Paul when he's overdone it, Joanna has helped him come to one of the most important decisions in his life. She was there when he went public about his decision to quit his role in the biggest show on TV. **It was true.** Paul was to leave EastEnders.

LIFE AFTER

TYPICALLY, Paul's mum spoke the most sense in the midst of the scandal about his exit from the soap. 'Paul is taking time out to enjoy himself with his girlfriend, have a rest and think about his future,' she said, as fans became worried sick that Paul was beginning to crack up himself, losing his mind under the immense pressure of becoming such a phenomenal success.

`'I've not been brought up to be like this,' he says, aware of the fact that appearing in a soap isn't just a job, it takes over your whole life. All the attention is nice, especially girls asking for an autograph. But I want to sleep for a week. I never have time for bed.'`

The news of him leaving the Square broke just as Paul was about to set off for Disneyland Paris with Joanna to help celebrate the theme park's fifth anniversary. 'I don't think I'll be in this business much longer,' he said. 'I don't watch EastEnders. I'll turn off because I think it's crap, not the programme, my acting. I sometimes cringe when I see it. I'm back on the set on Monday and hopefully they will give me a few more scripts and a good storyline.'

Paul needn't have worried about getting a few more scripts. The bosses at EastEnders are desperate to keep Joe in the cast because they know how many watch the show just to see him. If they don't like a character or an actor, they kill the part off. Not so with Joe Wicks – he is being kept alive. Paul can return to the show whenever he wants.

'He made the decision last September to stay for just another year,' says his mum. 'Paul isn't about to go mad. He just feels the time is right to leave. He wants to be known as an actor rather than a pin-up. I'd know if my own son was on the edge – he loves the acting but hates the fame. I realise a lot of people will be disappointed but this isn't the end of his career.'

The worry is that Paul will go down the plughole, like so many other ex-soap babes. There is a huge rollcall of them – Jason Donovan, Sean Maguire, Daniella Westbrook: none of them manage to find the same level of success once they leave the world of soap.

Lost World star Jeff Goldblum!

EastEnders

The big difference between Paul and these actors is that they acted like they believed they were stars, that they deserved and wanted to be famous even though they were no longer in the programmes that had made them celebrities. Paul has said again and again that he isn't happy with his success. He doesn't want to have this sort of fame, and so when he leaves EastEnders he isn't going to cash in on his role in the top TV soap. He is just going to act, and work on his own merits.

So, there will be no records by Paul. 'I would do if I could sing,' he says, 'but my cat Gizmo is better than I am. I'm going to have lessons because I'm so bloody awful.' At least twelve record companies have said they want to sign Paul up as a singer, but maybe they should follow his advice and get a contract ready for the cat instead. He has already shown his commitment to acting by the number of roles he had before he took the part in EastEnders. It wasn't his first role, and so it won't be his last.

everybody's fave posh pal Tamara Beckwith (doesn't Paul look happy?)

The SPICE GIRLS

PAUL HAD GREAT fun in the Spice Girls movie. His agent, Sylvia Young, who taught Baby Spice Emma Bunton at her drama school, said when he got the role, 'The Spice Girls are big fans of Paul and that's why he was asked. He has a small cameo part and will appear in several scenes.' Paul, who played a fan mad about the Spice Girls, found himself in a cast that included Roger Moore, Richard E. Grant, Richard Briers, and, of course, Mel B, Mel C, Emma, Geri and Victoria. Which is a better laugh than being stuck in Albert Square.

But Paul isn't claiming anything about his future. He is even modest enough to question his talents. 'To tell you the truth, I don't know if I can act,' he says. But we know it is acting that truly makes him happy.

Whatever he decides to do next, he can be sure it will be with the loyal support of thousands and thousands of devoted fans.

drop-dead gorgeous, talented, modest, caring, loves his mum...

...too good to be forgotten

Thank you

and goodbye

SOURCES

The Sun; TV Hits; Here!; OK! Magazine; The Mirror; The Sunday Mirror; The People;
The Star; The Daily Telegraph; The Independent; The Times.

This book is dedicated to TWT

Information

Paul Nicholls Fan Club

Paul Nicholls Web Site: http://.www.doyle.demon.co.uk/

Paul Nicholls

TA TA FOR NOW. . .